Who Was Gandhi?

Who Was Gandhi?

by Dana Meachen Rau

illustrated by Jerry Hoare

Penguin Workshop
An Imprint of Penguin Random House

For all the peacemakers—DMR

PENGUIN WORKSHOP
Penguin Young Readers Group
An Imprint of Penguin Random House LLC

Text copyright © 2014 by Dana Meachen Rau. Illustrations copyright © 2014 by Penguin Random House LLC. All rights reserved. Published by Penguin Workshop, an imprint of Penguin Random House LLC, 345 Hudson Street, New York, New York 10014. PENGUIN and PENGUIN WORKSHOP are trademarks of Penguin Books Ltd. WHO HQ & Design is a registered trademark of Penguin Random House LLC. Printed in the USA.

Library of Congress Control Number: 2014039150

ISBN 9780448482354   20 19 18 17 16 15 14

Contents

Who Was
Gandhi?

On March 12, 1930, sixty-year-old Mohandas Gandhi set out from his home in Ahmedabad, India, with seventy-eight men and women at his side. They walked 240 miles along winding, dusty roads. It took twenty-four days in the hot sun to reach the town of Dandi on the western coast. Gandhi spoke with villagers all along the way. By the end of his journey, several thousand people had joined him.

When the marchers arrived in Dandi, they prayed. The next morning, April 6, on the shore of the Arabian Sea, Gandhi picked up a lump of salt from the mud. By doing so, he broke the law. This peaceful act was powerful. It united many Indians against the unfair Salt Act laws. The Salt Acts stated that Indians could not gather, make, or sell their own salt.

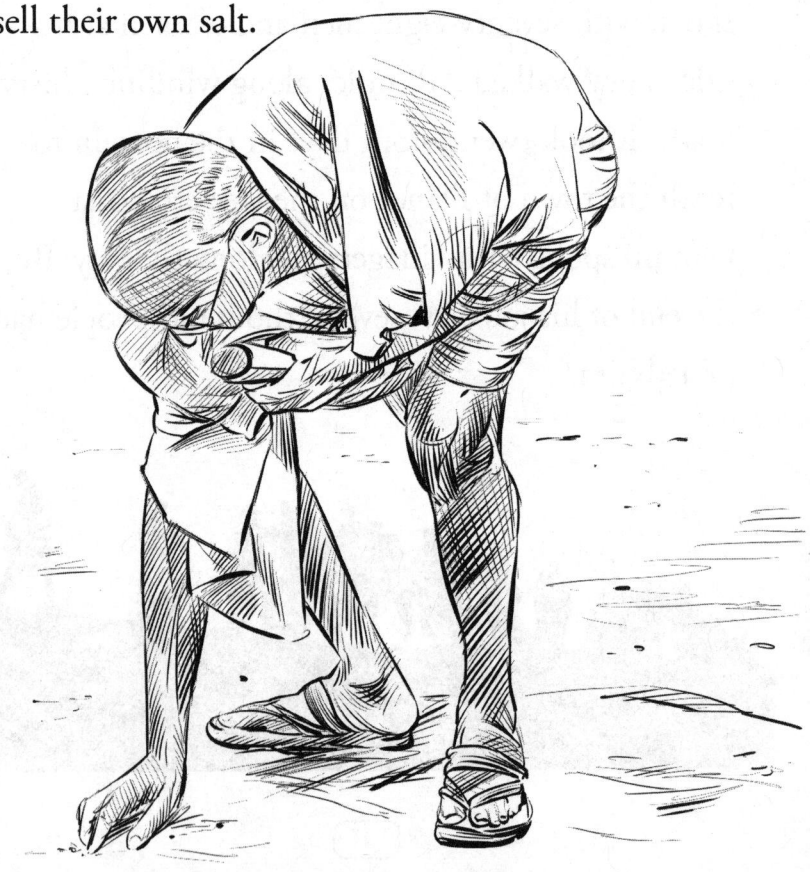

Instead they had to buy it from the British, who ruled India from 1858 to 1947. Salt was a basic need in Indian households to flavor food. After Gandhi's small but brave action, Indians all over the country began to gather and sell their own salt. Gandhi's Salt March started India on a path to freedom from British rule.

Mohandas Gandhi fought for freedom in India. But he did not fight with weapons. He believed words and actions were more powerful than violence. Above all, he had a simple message—to find truth through love and caring for others. People called him *Mahatma*, which means "Great Soul."

Chapter 1
Child Groom

Mohandas Karamchand Gandhi was born on October 2, 1869, in Porbandar, India. Porbandar was a small state on the western coast of a very large country. Mohandas, called Mohan by his family, grew up with his mother, father, two  half sisters from his father's previous marriages, oldest brother Laxmidas, sister Raliatbehn, and brother Karsandas. Mohan was the youngest.

His father, Karamchand, was the *diwan*, or
political leader, of Porbandar. The large family
lived well, with servants, in a three-story house.

Mohan grew up in a country with deep Hindu traditions. His mother, Putlibai, was especially religious. Every day, she went to the temple for worship. She prayed before meals. Sometimes she fasted, or gave up food, to show her devotion to God. During one period of four months during the rainy season, Putlibai said she would not eat until the sun came out. Gandhi later said,

"We children on those days would stand, staring at the sky, waiting to announce the appearance of the sun to our mother." His mother's devotion left a big impression on little Mohan. He saw her as a saint.

When Mohan turned seven, his family moved from Porbandar to the more inland city of Rajkot. At school, Mohan was an average student and extremely shy. "My books and my lessons were my sole companions," he said. As soon as school ended,

he would run home. He did not want to have to talk to anyone or risk someone making fun of him. Mohan was also very fearful as a child, and even into adulthood. He was afraid of thieves, snakes, ghosts, and most especially the dark.

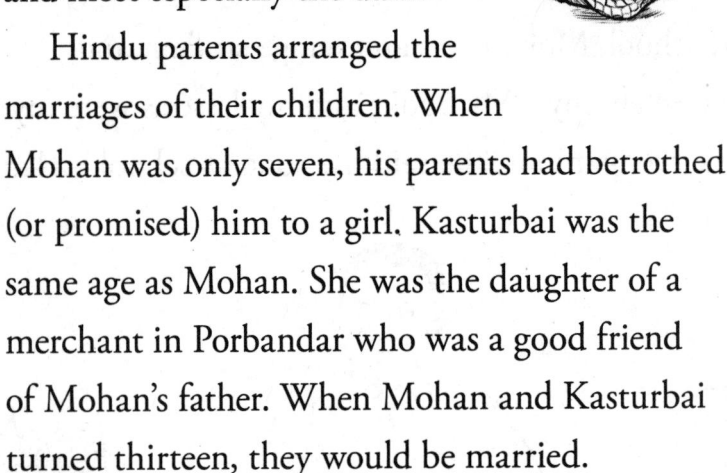

Hindu parents arranged the marriages of their children. When Mohan was only seven, his parents had betrothed (or promised) him to a girl. Kasturbai was the same age as Mohan. She was the daughter of a merchant in Porbandar who was a good friend of Mohan's father. When Mohan and Kasturbai turned thirteen, they would be married.

Later in life, Gandhi was very outspoken against the idea of child marriage. "I can see no moral argument in support of such a preposterously early marriage," he wrote. But during his own wedding, Gandhi enjoyed himself.

"Everything on that day seemed to me right and proper and pleasing," he said. The wedding was a huge party with many guests, colorful parades, and much celebration.

The bride and groom were fond of each other.

But marriage was not easy. Mohan and Kasturbai
had to learn how to be a husband and a wife.
The preparations, wedding, and new married life
interrupted Mohan's studies. He had to take a year
off before he returned to school.

RELIGION IN INDIA

HINDUISM IS STRONGLY LINKED TO THE PEOPLE AND CULTURE OF INDIA. THIS SET OF BELIEFS AND TRADITIONS DOES NOT EMBRACE ONE SINGLE GOD OR PROPHET. IT DOES INCLUDE THE BELIEF IN A UNIVERSAL SPIRIT, CALLED BRAHMAN, WHO CAN TAKE THE FORM OF MANY DIFFERENT GODS AND GODDESSES. HINDUISM IS DIVIDED INTO MANY SECTS AND SUBGROUPS, OF WHICH VAISHNAVISM AND SHAIVISM ARE THE LARGEST AND MOST POPULAR. GANDHI'S FAMILY MEMBERS WERE VAISHNAVA HINDUS. THEY WORSHIPPED THE GOD VISHNU.

IN GANDHI'S TIME, ABOUT ONE QUARTER OF THE POPULATION IN INDIA PRACTICED THE RELIGION ISLAM. ISLAM IS THE BELIEF IN ONE GOD, ALLAH. ITS FOLLOWERS ARE CALLED MUSLIMS AND THEY STUDY THE TEACHINGS OF THE PROPHET MUHAMMAD. MUSLIMS IN INDIA LIVED MOSTLY IN THE NORTH-EAST AND NORTHWEST OF THE COUNTRY UNTIL THE CREATION OF THE COUNTRY OF PAKISTAN IN 1947.

In high school, Mohan enjoyed pleasing his teachers. Outside of school, he tried to do the right thing as well. But one friend tried to get him to go against his beliefs. Mohan and his family were vegetarians. The friend told Mohan that eating meat would make him stronger and help him get over his fears. Mohan met his friend in secret by a river and tried meat for the first time. He got sick. He had nightmares. But he continued to eat meat for about a year. He didn't like lying to his family. He finally realized that his friend, and meat, were not good for him.

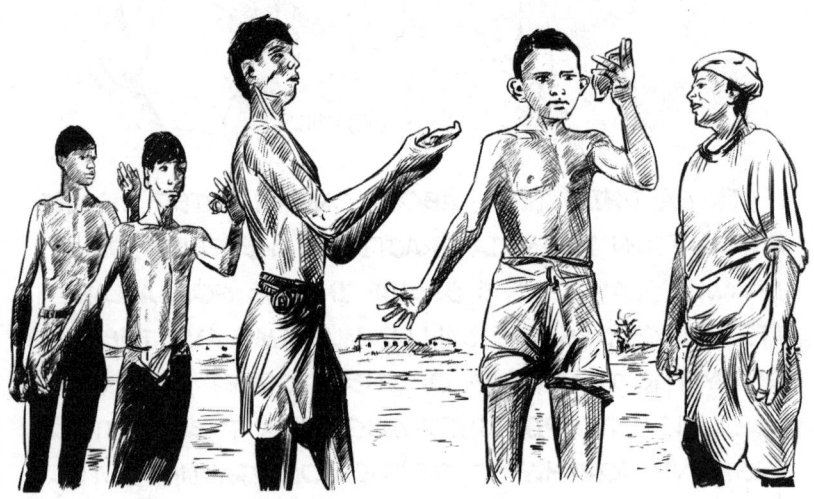

As a young man, Mohan had many responsibilities. This included caring for his sick father when he was not at school. His father died when Mohan was only sixteen. More sadness arrived when Mohan and Kasturbai's first baby passed away after only a few days.

In 1887, Mohan completed high school. He tried college, but found no interest in the lectures.

He didn't feel he was ready. After only one semester, he came home. A family friend suggested that Mohan go to England. He said it was easier to become a lawyer by attending school there. By studying law, he could become a *diwan* like his father. Mohan agreed.

It was not common for a young man from Rajkot to travel all the way to England for schooling. Gandhi had always been shy and fearful. Now he was headed for a new adventure far away from home.

THE BRITISH RAJ

IN 1600, THE EAST INDIA COMPANY (EIC) WAS FOUNDED BY LONDON MERCHANTS TRADING IN THE EAST INDIES. THE EIC TOOK OVER POLITICAL RULE IN INDIA BY DEFEATING THE BENGAL TROOPS AND THEIR FRENCH ALLIES IN THE BATTLE OF PLASSEY.

IN 1857, INDIAN TROOPS REBELLED AGAINST THE RULE OF THE EIC. AFTER THE REBELLION WAS DEFEATED, THE BRITISH RAJ (*RAJ* MEANS *RULE*) CONTROLLED THE COUNTRY. INDIAN PRINCES COULD STILL MAKE SOME LAWS FOR THEIR LOCAL AREAS. BUT A BRITISH VICEROY RULED THE WHOLE OF BRITISH INDIA FOR NEARLY ONE HUNDRED YEARS. MANY INDIANS WANTED EQUALITY AND WERE DISSATISFIED WITH BRITISH RULE. INDIA FINALLY BECAME INDEPENDENT IN 1947.

Chapter 2
London Lawyer

Mohandas Gandhi packed up and said good-bye to his family, including Kasturbai and their new baby son, Harilal. He headed to Bombay, India, where he would board a ship to London, England. Before he left Bombay,

the leaders of the Modh Bania caste called him into a meeting. Traveling overseas was against the caste's rules. They thought he would be tempted to break the rules of Hinduism while in England.

If he went, then he would be kicked out of the Modh Bania caste and treated as an untouchable. Courageously, Gandhi still went. He was only eighteen years old when he set sail from Bombay on September 4, 1888.

Gandhi had a hard time
fitting into a country so unlike
his own. "Everything was
strange—the people,
their ways, and even their
dwellings," he later wrote.
He tried hard to become
an "English gentleman."
He spent a lot of money
on a new suit, a top
hat, silver-tipped cane,
and leather gloves. He
took lessons in manners,
dance, French, and violin, like other Englishmen.
But none of that helped his loneliness and
homesickness.

Eating in London was hard for Gandhi, too.
Before he left India, he had promised his mother
that he would not eat meat. But finding vegetarian
meals in London was difficult. Since Gandhi was

shy, he didn't ask his hosts or waiters if they could make other choices for him. Vegetables tasted bland without the spices of home.

THE CASTE SYSTEM IN INDIA

IN TRADITIONAL HINDUISM AND INDIAN CULTURE, PEOPLE WERE DIVIDED INTO DIFFERENT SOCIAL LEVELS, OR CASTES.

RELIGIOUS PRIESTS AND TEACHERS MADE UP THE HIGHEST CASTE CALLED BRAHMANS. NEXT CAME KSHATRIYAS, THE WARRIORS AND ROYALTY. GANDHI'S FAMILY BELONGED TO THE NEXT CASTE—THE VAISHYAS—IN A SMALLER SUBGROUP CALLED THE MODH BANIAS. THE VAISHYA CASTE INCLUDED LANDOWNERS, MERCHANTS, AND FARMERS. THE SUDRAS MADE UP THE LOWEST CASTE. THESE WERE WORKERS AND CRAFTSMEN. PEOPLE COULD NOT MARRY MEMBERS OUTSIDE THEIR CASTE. THEY WERE NOT EVEN ALLOWED TO SHARE A MEAL WITH THEM!

ONE GROUP OF PEOPLE WERE CONSIDERED SO LOW, THEY WERE OUTSIDE THE CASTE SYSTEM. THEY WERE CALLED UNTOUCHABLES. UNTOUCHABLES HAD THE DIRTIEST JOBS, SUCH AS SWEEPING STREETS, CLEANING UP HUMAN WASTE, AND HANDLING GARBAGE. IN 1950, UNTOUCHABLES WERE GIVEN EQUAL RIGHTS UNDER LAW. TODAY, THE TERM *DALIT* REFERS TO THOSE ONCE CALLED UNTOUCHABLES. THE CASTE SYSTEM IS NO LONGER A PART OF THE EVERYDAY FABRIC OF MODERN INDIA. AND EVEN THOUGH DISCRIMINATION AGAINST *DALIT* INDIVIDUALS IS AGAINST THE LAW, MANY STILL FACE PREJUDICE, ESPECIALLY IN RURAL AREAS.

Gandhi took long walks through the city. On one of these walks, he came upon a vegetarian restaurant on Farringdon Street. Gandhi had finally found a place to eat. This discovery also introduced him to a whole community of vegetarians in London. He became a member of the London Vegetarian Society.

Gandhi completed his studies at University College and passed his law exams on June 10, 1891. The London Vegetarian Society held a farewell dinner in his honor. Gandhi had prepared a speech, but he was so shy and nervous that he couldn't read it. All he could get out was an uncomfortable "thank you."

Two days later, he set sail for home. He had only been in London for three years. But the lessons he learned about law, and about himself, would set him on his future path as a spiritual and political leader.

Chapter 3
An Unwelcome Visitor

Gandhi returned to India. Bombay Harbor greeted him with rough and choppy waters. Gandhi's older brother Laxmidas greeted him with sad news. Their mother had died while Gandhi was away.

Coming back home was not easy for Gandhi. His caste would not accept him. To please his brother, Gandhi agreed to bathe in the sacred Godavari River to wash away the sins of England.

He was then readmitted to his caste. But his home life was full of arguments with Kasturbai. Gandhi had tried to teach her new English traditions of cooking, eating, and dressing.

Gandhi went to find work in Bombay. But he soon found he was still too shy to be a lawyer. As he stood up to present his very first case, "My head was reeling, and I felt as though the whole court was doing likewise." He set up an office in Rajkot where he could work at his desk instead of in court.

Then Gandhi received some good news. A merchant from Porbandar was living in South Africa. He needed a lawyer for a court case there. The job would last one year. Gandhi decided to give it a try. Although he and his wife had recently welcomed a new baby boy named Manilal into their family, Gandhi left his wife and two young sons under Laxmidas's care and set out for Durban, South Africa, in April 1893.

A week after he arrived in South Africa, Gandhi traveled to Pretoria for his court case. He had a first-class ticket on the train. During the journey, the train stopped at the Maritzburg Station at about nine in the evening. A European

man entered the car. He did not like seeing an Indian man in first class. The man left and came back with a railway official. The official ordered Gandhi to go back to the third-class car.

Gandhi showed them his ticket. He refused

to leave the first-class car. The European man left again and came back with a policeman, who promptly kicked Gandhi off the train. Gandhi stood alone on the Maritzburg Station platform as the train pulled away.

The rest of the trip to Pretoria did not go much better. On a horse-drawn carriage, the white passengers did not want an Indian inside the coach with them. The coach leader told Gandhi to sit on the footboard—the small step that people used to get inside. "The insult was more than I could bear," Gandhi wrote.

When Gandhi finally arrived in Pretoria, he called the Indian community together for a meeting. He could no longer be timid. "My speech at this meeting may be said to have been the first public speech in my life," he said.

WHY DID SO MANY INDIANS LIVE IN SOUTH AFRICA?

WHEN GANDHI WAS A YOUNG MAN, THE BRITISH AND THE DUTCH GOVERNED DIFFERENT PARTS OF SOUTH AFRICA. CAPE COLONY AND NATAL WERE BRITISH COLONIES. DUTCH SETTLERS (THE BOERS) CONTROLLED THE TERRITORIES OF TRANSVAAL AND ORANGE FREE STATE. IN THE 1860S, MANY INDIANS CAME TO NATAL TO WORK ON THE SUGAR AND COFFEE PLANTATIONS. MORE INDIANS ARRIVED, WORKING AS MERCHANTS, AND INDIAN COMMUNITIES GREW. THE BRITISH SAW THEM AS A THREAT TO THEIR BUSINESSES. BY 1894 IN NATAL, INDIANS OUTNUMBERED WHITES 43,000 TO 40,000. SO TO CONTROL THE INDIAN POPULATION, THE BRITISH PASSED LAWS THAT LIMITED THEIR EQUALITY AND RIGHTS.

SOUTH AFRICA

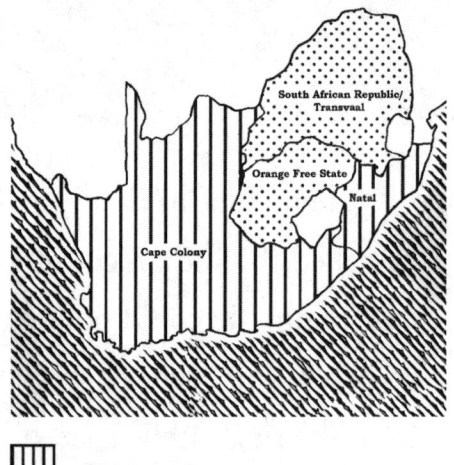

South African Republic/Transvaal

Orange Free State

Natal

Cape Colony

 BRITISH

 BOER

He shared his ideas about how Indians could improve their lives. He spoke about the need for fair treatment of Indians in South Africa. He knew he could go back to India. Or he could stand up for his rights, and the rights of Indians in South Africa. He decided to stay.

Chapter 4
Truth Force

When he finished his work on the court case in Pretoria, Gandhi felt that he still had a job to do. "Thus God laid the foundations of my life in South Africa, and sowed the seed of the fight for national self-respect," Gandhi wrote. In 1894, Gandhi set up the Natal Indian Congress so that Indians could be involved in government. Gandhi was becoming a leader in the Indian community.

Indians had very few rights in the colonies and territories in South Africa. They had to pay extra taxes. They could not walk on public footpaths. They could not go out after nine at night without a permit. They were told that the only legal marriages were between Christians, so their own marriages were considered invalid. They were not allowed to vote for their leaders.

Gandhi remembered one night when a police officer shoved him off a sidewalk: "Once, one of these men, without giving me the slightest warning, without even asking me to leave the footpath, pushed and kicked me into the street."

In 1896, after three years abroad, Gandhi returned to India. It was not easy for him to leave his important work with the Natal Indian

Congress behind. But Gandhi wanted his family to join him in South Africa. So Kasturbai, a nephew, and his two sons, now ages nine and five, made the return trip with him.

Once they arrived in Natal, Gandhi insisted they dress in uncomfortable clothing, such as stockings and shoes, and use utensils, such as knives and forks, like most Indians in South Africa. Kasturbai did her best to follow her husband's wishes in running her new South African household. But she did not always agree with him.

Gandhi and Kasturbai's family grew as they welcomed two more sons, Ramdas and Devdas. Gandhi kept working as a lawyer. But he never stopped working for the rights of Indian people living in South Africa.

In 1899, the Boer War began between the Dutch Boers and the British. Gandhi felt the best way to get the British to treat Indians well was to support the government. He put together an Indian ambulance corps with more than a thousand volunteers. They collected soldiers from the battlefield and nursed them back to health.

But this loyalty did not pay off. The British government continued to limit Indians' rights.

Gandhi found other ways to pull the Indian community of South Africa together. In 1903, he started work on a weekly journal called the *Indian Opinion*. He wrote articles about what

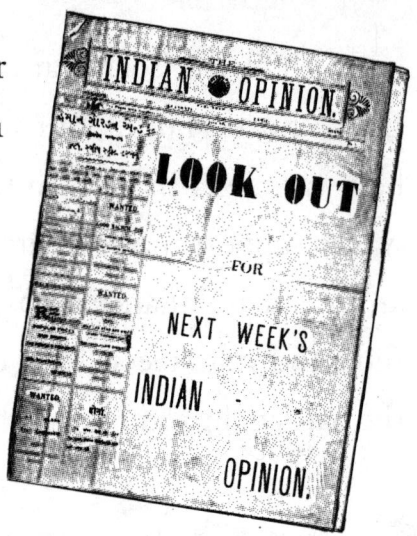

was happening in the government. He shared ideas for ways to treat sickness with natural medicines. He also wrote about the benefits of a vegetarian diet.

In South Africa, Gandhi developed his philosophy of life. He called it *satyagraha*—from the words *satya* (truth) and *agraha* (force). "Truth force" became the weapon he used against the unfair treatment of the Indian population. *Satyagraha* included ideas about noncooperation, nonviolence, and nonpossession.

SATYAGRAHA

NONCOOPERATION, OR CIVIL DISOBEDIENCE, MEANS NONVIOLENT WAYS OF BREAKING A LAW, IF THE LAW IS UNFAIR.

NONVIOLENCE MEANS DOING NO HARM AND LOVING OTHERS INSTEAD OF FIGHTING THEM.

NONPOSSESSION MEANS LIVING A SIMPLE LIFE WITH VERY FEW POSSESSIONS, AND USING ONLY WHAT ONE NEEDS, NEVER MORE.

In 1906, noncooperation was put to the test. In Transvaal, the government passed a law that Gandhi called the "Black Act." Indians had to register with the government. Every man, woman, and child over eight had to be fingerprinted and given certificates. At any time, police could stop Indians to prove they had registered, or even search their homes if they wished.

No other group was required to register in this way. "I saw nothing in it except hatred of Indians," Gandhi later wrote.

Gandhi urged Indians to use *satyagraha* and not register. Gandhi and many of his followers broke the law and were sent to jail. But Gandhi saw going to prison as an honorable thing to do. He was being courageous for what he believed in, even if it meant punishment.

While in South Africa, Gandhi started settlements where *satyagrahis* (those who followed *satyagraha*) could live together. Phoenix Settlement opened near Durban, in 1904. In 1909, Gandhi founded another settlement, about ten times the size of the Phoenix Settlement, near Johannesburg. He named it the Tolstoy Farm.

At these settlements, they practiced nonpossession by living a very simple life, owning only the most basic items. They studied and prayed. They farmed and gardened. Everyone worked and lived together as a community.

Gandhi urged Indians throughout South
Africa to practice nonviolence as well. Strikes,
or refusals to work, were a peaceful way to stand
up against unfairness in the workplace. Gandhi
organized a strike of Indian coal miners. Many
of them were put in jail for refusing to work, but
they did not use violence. Gandhi had shown the
lawmakers that Indians were willing to take action
against unfair treatment.

APARTHEID IN SOUTH AFRICA

INDIANS WERE NOT THE ONLY NONWHITE GROUP THAT FACED DISCRIMINATION IN SOUTH AFRICA. A SMALL WHITE MINORITY OF THE POPULATION WIELDED POWER OVER AN ENORMOUSLY LARGER BLACK AFRICAN POPULATION.

IN 1948, THE GOVERNMENT RULED THAT ALL RACES—WHITE, BLACK, INDIAN, AND COLORED (MIXED RACE)—HAD TO KEEP SEPARATE FROM EACH OTHER UNDER THE LAWS OF APARTHEID. APARTHEID MEANS *SEPARATENESS* IN THE AFRIKAANS LANGUAGE. PEOPLE OF DIFFERENT RACES COULD NOT LIVE IN THE SAME NEIGHBORHOODS,

GO TO THE SAME SCHOOLS OR HOSPITALS, RIDE THE SAME TRANSPORTATION, OR EVEN VISIT THE SAME BEACHES. WHITE PEOPLE HAD THE BEST SERVICES, WHILE PEOPLE OF COLOR OFTEN LIVED IN POVERTY AND WERE STRIPPED OF MANY RIGHTS.

NELSON MANDELA

APARTHEID DID NOT END UNTIL 1991.

IN 1994, WHEN PEOPLE OF ALL RACES COULD FINALLY VOTE IN SOUTH AFRICA, THE COUNTRY ELECTED ITS FIRST BLACK PRESIDENT, NELSON MANDELA.

After twenty years of hard work in South Africa, Gandhi had finally made a difference. The government passed the Indian Relief Act in July 1914, putting an end to unfair taxes and changing the marriage law to include all faiths.

Gandhi felt his work was done in South Africa. He had only planned to stay one year, but he ended up staying for twenty-one!

Gandhi had arrived in South Africa as a shy, young lawyer. Now in his forties, he left as a well-known leader. He would now bring his "truth force" back home to India.

Chapter 5
Mahatma in India

Gandhi had lived away from India for more than twenty years. But his work in South Africa was well-known in India. He had written pamphlets that had been distributed there. Newspapers, in both England and India, had reported stories of his work in South Africa. His home country greeted him like a hero.

Rabindranath Tagore, a famous poet of the time, called Gandhi *Mahatma*, which means "Great Soul." Indians started calling him Mahatma to show their great respect for him.

Gandhi came home with a mission. He wanted India to govern itself. He wanted to show the British Raj that Indians would be loyal to them. He urged Indians to be confident and act fairly. He urged them to show respect to the British and not treat them as an enemy. In return, he hoped the government would give India its independence. Gandhi also wanted Indians to look at the unfair parts of their own traditions, such as the caste system and treatment of untouchables. He wanted to put *satyagraha* to work in India, too.

He created a settlement that was similar to the Phoenix and Tolstoy Farm communities, the Satyagraha Ashram. The settlement was on the Sabarmati River near the city of Ahmedabad.

Gandhi had carefully chosen this location.
Ahmedabad was a center for the textile industry.
The people of Gandhi's ashram spun yarn and
wove cloth. The businesspeople of Ahmedabad

welcomed the ashram and collected money to help support it. Opened on May 25, 1915, the Satyagraha Ashram members lived like one large family. Besides spinning yarn, they farmed and grew fruit trees. They read and studied and prayed. They lived a simple life without many possessions.

Gandhi called the untouchables of India *harijans*, which means "children of God." He wished to treat them like any other Indians. But even members of the ashram, who agreed with most of Gandhi's beliefs, did not always agree with Gandhi's teachings about untouchables. In September 1915, an untouchable couple and their baby daughter wanted to join the ashram. Gandhi accepted them. Some members objected and left the ashram. Even Kasturbai was upset.

She refused to work in the kitchen alongside the untouchable woman. The textile owners who had donated money for the running of the ashram refused to continue their support.

Then one day, one of the most powerful Hindu businessmen in Ahmedabad drove to the ashram. He gave Gandhi enough money to keep the community going for at least another year. Gandhi was pleased. The fact that traditional Hindus were

willing to help his efforts at the ashram made Gandhi believe that change was coming soon. Kasturbai looked to Gandhi as her leader and stood by him.

Gandhi also cared for poor people in the villages that surrounded the ashram. He opened schools in the villages. He taught the peasants that good hygiene could help to keep away sickness and disease. He gave advice to farmers.

Gandhi even organized workers in the factories of Ahmedabad to strike against unfair employers without using violence. The work stoppage of the strikes proved that nonviolence could work for change.

In 1914, World War I broke out in Europe. Since Britain was involved in the fighting, that meant India was, too. Gandhi supported the war, even though he believed in nonviolence. Once again, he thought that supporting Britain might help India gain its independence. "We must perceive," he wrote in a letter to the viceroy, "that if we serve to save the [British] Empire, we have in that very act secured [Indian] Home Rule." Many Indians volunteered for the British Army and helped them win the war.

WHO'S ABSENT?

Is it you?

But Britain did not reward India with self-rule. When the war ended, the government passed even harsher laws against the Indians! The Rowlatt Acts of 1919 made it against the law for *any* group to organize against the government. Gandhi knew this law was unfair. It was time to use truth force again.

Gandhi called for a *hartal*, or strike, to protest the Rowlatt Acts, on April 6, 1919. Word spread through newspapers and local meetings throughout India. For one day, Indians would not go to work. Shops, railways, and farms stopped for the day. Many Indians gathered peacefully during the *hartal* to spend the day fasting and praying. Gandhi was pleased with the result. "The whole of India from one end to the other, towns as well as villages, observed a complete *hartal* on that day. It was a most wonderful spectacle," he said.

But in some cities, the *hartal* did not go well. Gandhi received news that some Indians had burned buildings and ripped up railroad tracks. In Amritsar, a number of British men were killed. Whether the Indians were peaceful or violent, police treated them the same. They beat the Indians with their brass-tipped sticks called *lathis*.

Gandhi was very upset. This was not how he planned the *hartal* to go. He realized all of India was not yet ready for *satyagraha*. "I had expected better things . . . ," Gandhi said, ". . . and I felt I was a sharer in their guilt."

After the *hartal*, British officers worried there might be more outbreaks of violence. On April 12, 1919, General Dyer, the British officer in charge of the troops in the city of Amritsar, issued a proclamation to the citizens. It stated that no meetings of Indians were allowed.

The next day, April 13, was a holiday. Vaisakhi Day was the beginning of the religious new year for many Indians.

GENERAL DYER

62

A crowd of about ten thousand to twenty thousand people gathered to celebrate in Jallianwala Bagh square in the center of the city. The square had one narrow entrance, and was surrounded on all sides by high buildings. The crowd had not yet heard of the ban on Indian gatherings. They peacefully listened to a speaker on a podium.

General Dyer arrived. He brought along ninety soldiers and two armored cars. They blocked the entrance. Dyer ordered his troops to fire their guns on the unarmed crowd of men, women, and children.

People panicked and tried to flee. But there was no way out. The firing lasted ten minutes. The official British reports stated 379 people were killed, and 1,137 wounded. But Indians believe it was many more.

REMEMBRANCE

TODAY, JALLIANWALA BAGH IS A PUBLIC GARDEN. IN 1951, A MEMORIAL WAS BUILT IN THE GARDEN TO HONOR THE MANY INDIANS WHO LOST THEIR LIVES IN THE MASSACRE. VISITORS CAN SEE THE TALL WALLS ON EACH SIDE, SOME STILL DOTTED WITH BULLET HOLES. A FLAME BURNS TO REMEMBER ALL THOSE WHO LOST THEIR LIVES ON APRIL 13, 1919.

General Dyer saw the incident as a way to teach the Indians a lesson: that the government made the laws, and the people had to follow.

Gandhi was horrified. Many innocent Indians had died in the massacre. Gandhi would no longer be loyal to the British government. It was time for him to fight back.

Chapter 6
Nonviolent Noncooperation

The peaceful gathering in Amritsar had turned into a violent massacre. The Indian people now knew they could not rally against the government without fearing for their lives.

Gandhi faced this fear bravely. He would stand up to the British government with his own weapon of noncooperation. He urged the Indian people to stand with him as well. But they would have to be willing to face the punishment that came with breaking the law. Gandhi spread the word in speeches at political meetings and through articles in his magazine, *Young India*.

In 1920, Gandhi became the leader of the Indian National Congress (INC), which adopted his nonviolent noncooperation campaign as its own. The INC was becoming a strong political voice for the Indian people.

Strikes had been one nonviolent way to stand up against unfair laws. Boycotts were another. A boycott is a refusal to buy certain items. In India, the British controlled the manufacture and sale of cloth. Gandhi urged Indians to refuse to buy the British cloth, so that the British cloth industry would make less money and profit in India.

Instead, Gandhi supported Indians making their own cloth. By making cloth at home, the Indian community would keep more money instead of paying the British. Gandhi believed that spinning and weaving would help give Indians freedom from British control.

Gandhi himself vowed to spin thread every day. He even stayed up late into the night to spin if he had to. He started wearing *khadi* (clothing made of hand-spun cloth) with sandals, and a shawl in cooler weather. To Gandhi, the spinning wheel was not only a tool to make thread. It became a national symbol for India's independence. In fact, a spinning wheel was originally part of the design for the flag of the new country.

GANDHI'S NONVIOLENT WEAPONS

STRIKE: REFUSAL TO WORK

BOYCOTT: REFUSAL TO BUY GOODS

FAST: REFUSAL TO EAT

It was not always easy for Gandhi to spread his message in a country covering more than 1.5 million square miles! Leaving his wife behind at the ashram, Gandhi reached out to the rest of India.

Most of the poor in India lived in villages that were hard to reach by train or car. So Gandhi did a lot of walking.

Of his journeys throughout India, he said "You will never get to know the real India until you get out of Delhi, Bombay, and the other cities and see how the overwhelming mass of Indians, half-starved and in rags, pass their lives in their

wretched huts in half a million villages, toiling
from dawn to dark in the nearby sun-parched
fields to wrest a little food from a worn-out soil."

Gandhi listened to their concerns, and the villagers of India treated him like a saint. They called him *Bapu*, which means father.

At home, Gandhi wanted his sons to be good examples. His oldest son, Harilal, had already moved away from the family. But his other sons supported his cause. Manilal had gone back to South Africa and became the editor of the *Indian Opinion* to continue the work Gandhi had begun. Both Ramdas and Devdas supported their father in India and worked closely with him.

In March 1922, Gandhi was arrested for urging others to break the law, which is known as *sedition*. At his trial, Gandhi explained that he had once been a loyal British subject. But because the British laws were so unfair to Indian and all nonwhite people, he refused to cooperate. He pled guilty and was willing to take the punishment—a sentence of six years at the Yeravda Central Prison in Poona.

Gandhi did not mind prison. In fact, he welcomed the time to be alone. He rested, read, and studied. And he continued to spin daily.

In January 1924, however, he had an attack of appendicitis. He had to be rushed to a hospital. After serving less than two years, the court officials decided Gandhi's sentence had been long enough. He was released from prison in February 1924.

Gandhi went right back to work uniting
India. This time, he focused his attention on
the split between the Hindus and Muslims.

These two religious groups had a long history of disagreement in India. They often fought violently with each other over differences in the religious beliefs. Gandhi used another of his peaceful weapons—fasting—to try to get Hindus and Muslims to listen to each other. In September 1924, he stopped eating and started a three-week fast. He only drank water. He grew weaker and weaker.

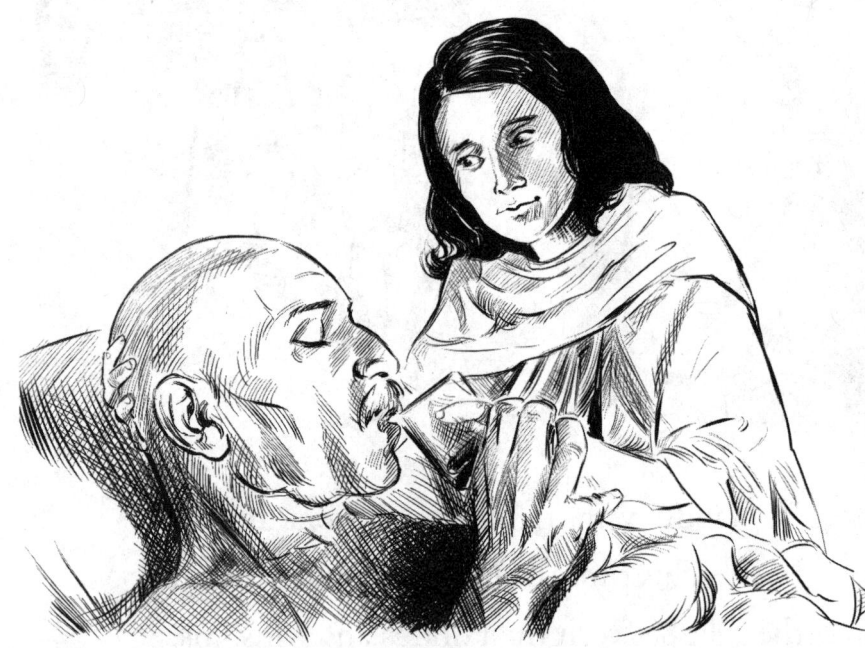

The Hindus and Muslims decided to put aside their differences so he would break his fast and begin eating again. They did not want Gandhi to suffer anymore. The religious leaders agreed to try to live peacefully with each other.

On March 12, 1930, Gandhi left his ashram in Ahmedabad with a group of seventy-eight people. They headed south for a march to the sea that would take almost a month. The weather was unbearably hot, so they traveled during the cooler parts of the day: early morning and evening. Villagers sprinkled the dusty dirt roads with water to keep the dust down. They threw leaves and flower petals on the path to make walking easier.

Along the 240-mile journey, Gandhi picked up hundreds of followers. The group grew to several thousand, a mix of young and old, men and women, Muslim, Christian, Hindu, and untouchable. A few local newspapermen followed along at first. As the news spread and the crowds grew,

newspapers all around the world featured articles
about the march on their front pages.

THE SALT ACTS

TAXATION OF SALT HAD OCCURRED IN INDIA SINCE THE BRITISH EAST INDIA COMPANY BEGAN EXPORTING SALT IN THE 1600S.

THE SALT ACTS, AS THESE TAXES WERE KNOWN, MADE IT AGAINST THE LAW FOR ANYONE TO MAKE THEIR OWN SALT FROM SEAWATER. THIS ENSURED THAT THE BRITISH WOULD MAKE HUGE PROFITS FROM THE TAXES ON SALT—EVEN FROM THE INDIAN PEOPLE WHO LIVED WHERE THE SALT WAS HARVESTED! ALL INDIANS WERE FORCED TO BUY SALT FROM THE BRITISH. THIS WAS ESPECIALLY UNFAIR TO THE POOR OF INDIA WHO COULD NOT AFFORD IT.

On April 5, twenty-four days after Gandhi left the ashram, he arrived in Dandi on the coast of the Gulf of Cambay, an inlet of the Arabian Sea. That night, he and his followers prayed on the beach.

The next morning, Gandhi waded into the water, to bathe in the Hindu tradition. Then he walked onto the beach and picked up a lump of salt in defiance of the Salt Acts.

Within a week, tens of thousands of Indians along the country's many miles of coastline broke the law by collecting seawater to make and sell salt.

Indians gathered in the cities, where police beat the crowds with *lathis*. Thousands of people were arrested. On May 5, Gandhi, too, was arrested and jailed, along with other political leaders, including Jawaharlal Nehru, an INC member and trusted friend.

NEHRU, GANDHI, AND PATEL

The British finally realized that "Mahatma" Gandhi was a powerful force in India. He had unified a whole nation with his campaign of nonviolent noncooperation.

Chapter 7
Quitting India

The British had to listen to Gandhi after seeing how he had united the Indian people. They also had to face the harsh reaction of the rest of the world. The government received telegrams from all over the world demanding that Gandhi and the other INC members be released from jail. Lord Irwin, the viceroy in India, met with Gandhi. Together, they reached a truce. Gandhi would call off the civil-disobedience campaign, all prisoners would be released, and Indians could make their own salt.

Gandhi was ready to represent the Indian National Congress in London for the Round Table Conference of 1931. He would speak in support of an independent India.

Gandhi traveled to London with his son Devdas and a few other supporters. While in London, Gandhi did not want to stay at a fancy hotel. Instead he was a guest at a friend's house, and spent his days walking in the slums, talking with the poor people of London. While other political leaders wore suits, he wore his *khadi* and sandals. He even had tea with King George V and Queen Mary of England in his simple clothing.

The Times
LONDON, SATURDAY, MARCH 14, 1931

By now, Gandhi was world famous. His arrival made the front-page news. Thousands came to get a glimpse of him. Londoners enjoyed this friendly, kind-mannered little man with big ideas.

But he did not have success with his plans for independence. Within a week after returning to India, the government arrested him and other Indian leaders, for starting another noncooperation campaign.

Gandhi still fought for the Indian people while in jail in Yeravda. The British government was planning to keep the untouchables separate in courts and within government systems. Gandhi did not want the untouchables to be considered separate from the rest of Indian society. To protest this law, Gandhi announced that he would not eat until he died. Kasturbai, who was being held at Sabarmati Prison, was transferred to Yeravda Prison to be with her husband. Doctors examined Gandhi and felt certain he was about to die.

The government quickly agreed to Gandhi's terms and he ended his fast. They did not want to risk the death of such a famous and beloved man.

In 1939, the British entered World War II. Gandhi was upset that the British had not even discussed it with the Indian National Congress.

He told British government officials that India would only cooperate if Britain promised them independence. Gandhi wondered why India should fight for others' freedoms when Indians did not have their own freedoms under British law.

Gandhi was determined to see India become independent from the British. In 1942, he started a "Quit India" movement. He wanted Britain to leave the country and let India's people govern themselves. He told the British if they agreed to leave, then India would support Britain in the war and fight on their side.

Gandhi wanted his Quit India campaign to be

nonviolent, as always. But it spun out of his control. All over India, many Indians rioted. The British government blamed Gandhi and arrested him with Nehru, Kasturbai, and about fifty other followers.

Prison was frustrating for Gandhi. He could not speak to the press or write letters and articles. And then Kasturbai became sick with bronchitis. Gandhi's beloved wife died in prison on February 22, 1944, in his arms. They had been married for more than sixty years.

Gandhi grew ill and weak from malaria. Officials agreed to let him out of jail early in May 1944. He went to stay with a friend in Bombay to rest and gain back his strength. During his lifetime, he had spent a total of nearly six and a half years in jail.

World War II ended in May 1945. Great Britain had spent so much money fighting the war, it no longer had the resources to keep India under its rule. Finally, the British offered India its independence. Gandhi, Nehru, Vallabhbhai Patel, and other Indian leaders met to work out their new form of government. The British sent representatives to transfer power from Britain to India. But the Hindus and Muslims could still not settle their differences. Dividing the country into two (India for Hindus and Pakistan in the northwest for Muslims) seemed to be the only solution.

At midnight on August 15, 1947, India became

independent. Nehru would be its new prime minister. Gandhi was sitting on a wooden cot in a hut in Calcutta when India finally became its own nation.

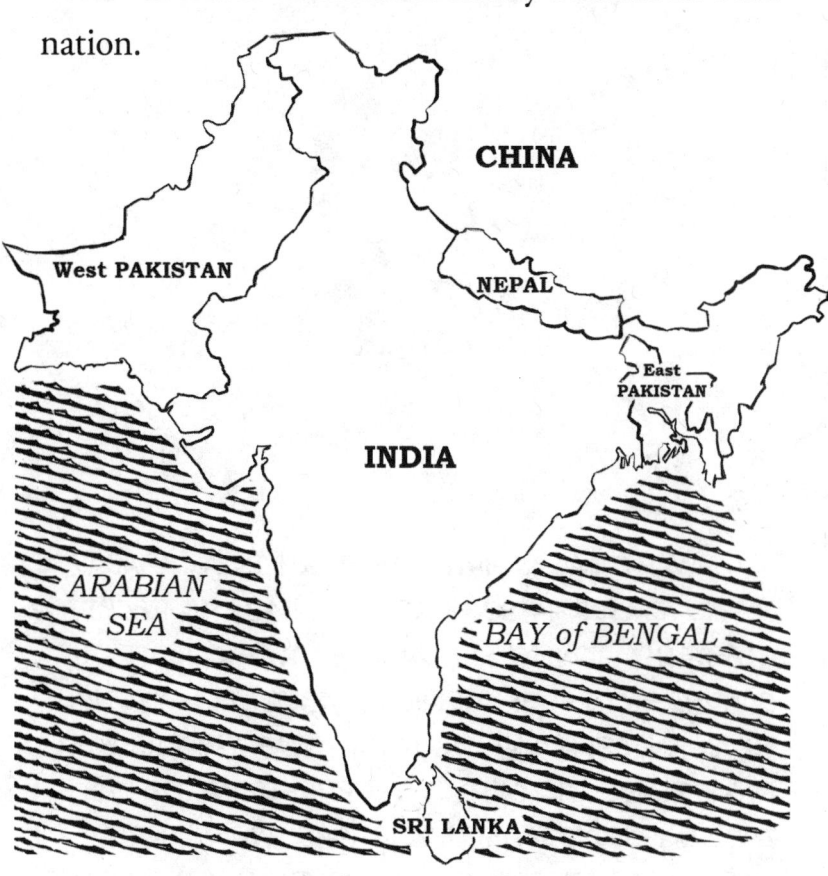

All over India, people celebrated. Gandhi did not.

JAWAHARLAL NEHRU

JAWAHARLAL NEHRU WAS BORN IN ALLAHABAD ON NOVEMBER 14, 1889. LIKE GANDHI, HE RECEIVED HIS EDUCATION IN ENGLAND. HE WAS ONE OF GANDHI'S CLOSEST AIDES. HE BELIEVED STRONGLY IN AN INDEPENDENT INDIA AND WAS IMPRISONED MANY TIMES. HE SERVED AS PRESIDENT OF THE INC IN 1929, 1936, 1937, AND 1946. WHEN INDIA GAINED ITS INDEPENDENCE, NEHRU BECAME PRIME MINISTER, AND CONTINUED IN THIS ROLE UNTIL HIS DEATH IN 1964.

Chapter 8
A Light Has Gone Out

Gandhi had helped bring about independence. His weapons to free India had been love and truth. But Gandhi's hopes could not solve all of the country's problems. Hindus and Muslims clashed violently.

After the creation of Pakistan, millions of Muslims and Hindus had to move from their homes and cross the new border between the countries. Muslims in East Punjab had to flee to the west (the new Pakistan). Hindus had to move from west to east. Throughout 1947, violent massacres occurred between the groups. Hundreds of thousands of people were killed.

In big cities, such as Calcutta and Delhi, riots continued between the religious groups as well.

On January 13, 1948, Gandhi began a fast to try to get them to stop. He did not even drink water. He was in pain. But even curled up in bed, he led a prayer meeting. Gandhi's prayers were broadcast by radio and heard over all of India. After five days of negotiations, both Hindu and Muslim political leaders came before Gandhi and agreed to his terms. They did not want to see Gandhi suffer.

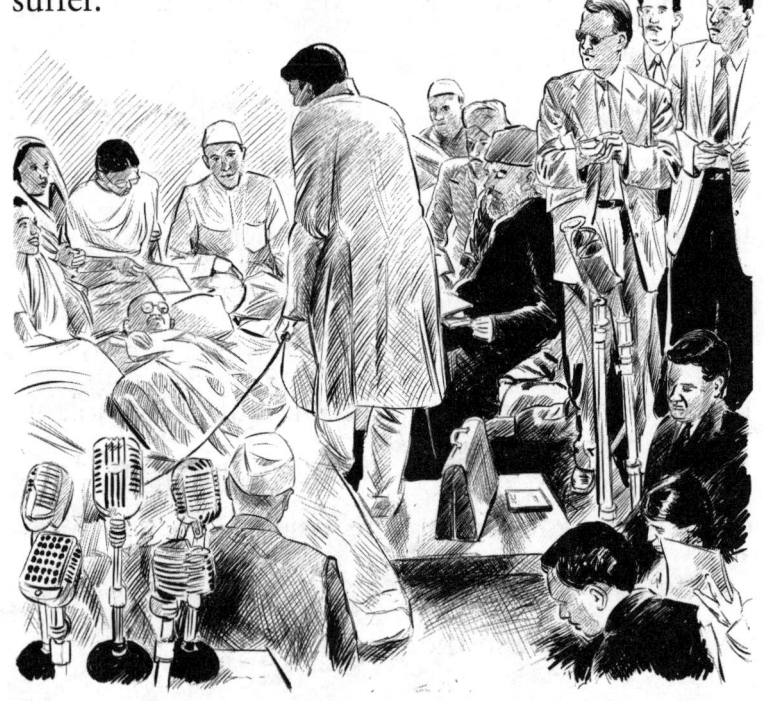

Gandhi was still concerned for the leadership of India. Nehru was now prime minister, and Patel was deputy prime minister. But the two did not always get along. Gandhi wrote to Nehru to tell him that they must work together. On January 30, 1948, he met with Patel and urged him to do the same.

He left the dinner with Patel to lead a prayer meeting. He was now almost eighty years old.

His body was weak from his fasts and he had trouble walking, so he leaned on two of his followers for support. He walked out to greet the crowd of about five hundred.

Most Indians looked up to Gandhi as a spiritual and political leader. But there was an extreme Hindu group that blamed Gandhi for the death of so many Hindus. They were upset that Gandhi had reached out to the Muslims.

As Gandhi headed toward the platform, Nathuram Godse, a Hindu extremist, pushed through the crowd to get close to him. He bowed before Gandhi. Then he took out a pistol. He fired three shots right into Gandhi's chest. Gandhi fell to the ground.

The evening Gandhi died, Prime Minister Nehru said in a radio address, "The light has gone out of our lives and there is darkness everywhere."

The people of India, and people everywhere, mourned the loss of one of the world's greatest teachers. Gandhi had been a light to the people of India and to the world. His light continued to shine as India grew as an independent nation. He proved that truth and love are the strongest forces for change.

TIMELINE OF GANDHI'S LIFE

1869 — Mohandas Karamchand Gandhi is born in Porbandar, India, on October 2

1883 — Gandhi and Kasturbai marry

1893 — Gandhi arrives in South Africa to practice law

1894 — Gandhi sets up the Natal Indian Congress to help give Indians a voice in government

1904 — Gandhi starts the Phoenix Settlement near Durban, housing the *Indian Opinion* weekly journal

1906 — Gandhi urges Indians to practice noncooperation by not registering in protest to an unfair law

1909 — Gandhi starts the Tolstoy Farm near Johannesburg

1915 — Gandhi opens the Satyagraha Ashram on the banks of the Sabarmati River in India

1919 — Gandhi organizes a *hartal* against unfair laws. It is soon followed by a massacre of innocent Indians in the city of Amritsar on April 13

1920 — The Indian National Congress (INC) adopts Gandhi's nonviolent noncooperation campaign

1922 — Gandhi is arrested and jailed for sedition (urging others to break the law)

1930 — Gandhi leads the Salt March in protest of the unfair government Salt Acts

1931 — Gandhi represents the INC at the Round Table Conference in London

1942 — Gandhi starts the "Quit India" movement, urging Britain to leave India so they can govern themselves

1944 — Gandhi's wife, Kasturbai, dies on February 22

1947 — India is declared independent on August 15

1948 — Gandhi is assassinated on January 30

TIMELINE OF THE WORLD

Abraham Lincoln signs the Emancipation Proclamation to abolish slavery in the United States	1863
The first transcontinental railroad is completed in America, connecting the nation from east to west	1869
Thomas Edison invents the electric light bulb	1879
The Eiffel Tower is built as the entrance for the World's Fair in Paris	1889
Italian inventor Guglielmo Marconi sends the first communication over radio signals	1895
Robert Peary and Matthew Henson discover the North Pole	1909
World War I begins	1914
The United States passes the Nineteenth Amendment, giving women the right to vote	1920
Archaeologist Howard Carter discovers the tomb of Egyptian pharaoh Tutankhamen	1922
World War II begins	1939
The official government policy of apartheid (a separation of whites and nonwhites) begins in South Africa	1948
Dr. Martin Luther King Jr. gives his famous "I Have a Dream" speech in Washington, DC, to speak out for equal rights of black Americans	1963
Mother Teresa is awarded the Nobel Peace Prize for her work with the poor in India	1979

BIBLIOGRAPHY

Brown, Judith M. **Gandhi: Prisoner of Hope**. New Haven, Connecticut: Yale University Press, 1989.

Fischer, Louis. **Gandhi: His Life and Message for the World**. New York: New American Library, 1954.

Gandhi, Mohandas K. **Gandhi: An Autobiography: The Story of My Experiments With Truth**. Boston: Beacon Press, 1993.*

Lelyveld, Joseph. **Great Soul: Mahatma Gandhi and His Struggle With India**. New York: Alfred A. Knopf, 2011.

New York Times, On This Day, January 31, 1948. "Mohandas K. Gandhi: The Indian Leader at Home and Abroad." http://www.nytimes.com/learning/general/onthisday/bday/1002.html. Accessed May 29, 2013.

Shirer, William L. **Gandhi: A Memoir**. New York: Washington Square Press, 1979.

* Gandhi's autobiography was first published in 1927 and 1929 in two volumes. The English translation first appeared in *Young India* as a series of articles. Then the English translation was collected into book form in 1940.